# Cupids, Cherubs and Nymphs

### Marty Noble

D0763200

DOVER PUBLICATIONS, INC.
Mineola, New York

# NOTE

Precious cupids, cherubs, and nymphs cavort in this enchanting collection of illustrations. These winged, heavenly creatures will add charm and grace to any graphic arts or crafts projects. You may scan these images of delightful cherubs into your computer and use them as they appear here, or they can be reproduced in larger or smaller sizes for a variety of applications.

Artist Marty Noble has adapted these ethereal designs from a multitude of different sources, including famous paintings, book decorations, and Renaissance etchings and engravings. Amid flowers, butterflies, and musical instruments, these cherubim are sure to lift your spirits and brighten your day. Captions identifying the images are provided where possible.

*Copyright*

Copyright © 2003 by Dover Publications, Inc.
All rights reserved.

*Bibliographical Note*

*Cupids, Cherubs and Nymphs* is a new work, first published by Dover Publications, Inc., in 2003.

DOVER *Pictorial Archive* SERIES

This book belongs to the Dover Pictorial Archive Series. You may use the designs and illustrations for graphics and crafts applications, free and without special permission, provided that you include no more than four in the same publication or project. (For permission for additional use, please write to Permissions Department, Dover Publications, Inc., 31 East 2nd Street, Mineola, N.Y. 11501.)

However, republication or reproduction of any illustration by any other graphic service, whether it be in a book or in any other design resource, is strictly prohibited.

*Library of Congress Cataloging-in-Publication Data*

Noble, Marty, 1948–
    Cupids, cherubs, and nymphs / Marty Noble.
        p. cm.—(Dover design library) (Dover pictorial archive series)
    ISBN 0-486-42836-2 (pbk.)
    1. Cupid (Roman deity)—Art. 2. Angels in art. 3. Nymphs (Greek deities) in art. 4. Decoration and ornament. I. Title. II. Series. III. Series: Dover pictorial archive series.

NK1590.C84N63 2003
745.4—dc21

                                                                    2002041608

Manufactured in the United States of America
Dover Publications, Inc., 31 East 2nd Street, Mineola, N.Y. 11501

Phoenix and cupids,
printer's engraving,
1500s (Renaissance)

Plantin decoration
(Renaissance)

1

*The Sistine Madonna* (detail) by Raphael

3

Plantin decoration
(Renaissance)

*Aurora* (detail) by Guido Reni

Adapted from engraving
on steel (Renaissance)

Printer's engraving, German,
1500s (Renaissance)

Etching design
(Renaissance)

Printer's mark,
Paris, 1500s
(Renaissance)

Detail, adapted from painting by Bouguereau

Detail from title page design
by Hans Holbein (Renaissance)

Design from French decorative panel

7

*The Coronation of the Virgin* (detail)
by Guido Reni (1626)

9

Cupids in intertwined
volutes,
from series of passe-
partout border in
the Venetian edition of
*Orlando Furioso*

10

German book decoration, 1530

Detail from *Lunette Fresco with Angels*, School of Montecassino (Italian)

*Christ Served by the Angels* (detail)
by Jacques de Stella (1600s)

14

*The Two Trinities*
(detail) by Murillo

16

Printer's mark,
1500s (Renaissance)

Ornament from 16th-century Italian manuscript

Albrecht Dürer

19

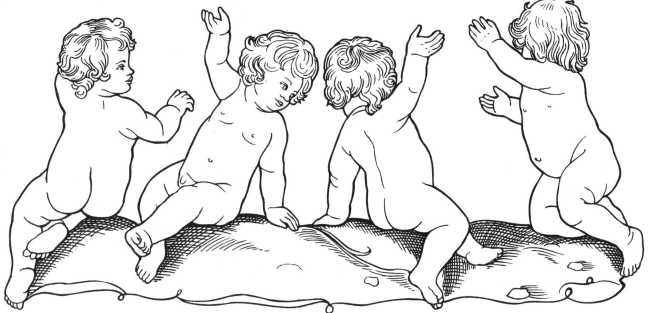

Interior decoration, France,
17th century

Side panel design by Albrecht Dürer

Detail from German
ornamental panel

25

BORDER: German design from a work printed in 1559

*God the Father Appearing to*
*St. Catherine* (detail)
by Fra Bartolomeo